Hurricanes

CHRISTY STEELE

Raintree

Nature on the Rampage

www.raintreepublishers.co.uk
Visit our website to find out more information about **Raintree** books.

To order:
☎ Phone 44 (0) 1865 888112
🖷 Send a fax to 44 (0) 1865 314091
🖳 Visit the Raintree Bookshop at www.raintreepublishers.co.uk to browse our catalogue and order online.

First published in Great Britain by Raintree Publishers, Halley Court, Jordan Hill, Oxford, OX2 8EJ, part of Harcourt Education.
Raintree is a registered trademark of Harcourt Education Ltd.

Consultant: Frank Lepore, National Hurricane Center, USA

Editor: Isabel Thomas
Cover Design: Jo Sapwell and Michelle Lisseter
Production: Jonathan Smith

Originated by Dot Gradations
Printed and bound in China and Hong Kong by South China

ISBN 1 844 21210 6
07 06 05 04 03
10 9 8 7 6 5 4 3 2 1

British Library Cataloguing in Publication Data
Steele, Christy
Hurricanes. – (Nature on the Rampage)
1.Hurricanes – Juvenile Literature
551.5'52
A catalogue for this book is available from the British Library

Acknowledgements
The publishers would like to thank the following for permission to reproduce photographs:
Archive Photos/Reuters/Ana Martinez, p. **4**; Reuters/Rick Wilking, p. **16**; Digital Stock, pp. **10, 20, 22, 24, 27, 29**; Photo Network/Jeff Greenberg, p. **18**
Photophile, p. **12**

Cover photograph by NASA

Every effort has been made to contact copyright holders of any material reproduced in this book. Any omissions will be rectified in subsequent printing if notice is given to the publishers.

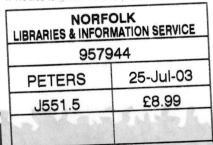

Contents

How hurricanes start 5

Hurricanes in history 13

Hurricanes today 19

Hurricanes and science 25

Glossary 30

Addresses and Internet sites 31

Index 32

How hurricanes start

Hurricanes are some of nature's strongest storms. They are also known as **tropical** cyclones or typhoons. Hurricanes are made up of bands of thunderstorms. Powerful winds and the Earth's spinning movement make the bands of thunderstorms rotate, or spin around the centre of the storm.

Hurricanes are large storms. They may be up to 16 kilometres (10 miles) high and 1600 kilometres (1000 miles) wide. Hurricanes can blow down trees and houses. Rain from hurricanes can cause floods.

◀ **Hurricane winds can blow down trees.**

Naming hurricanes and cyclones

In 1978 scientists decided to name hurricanes. Scientists pick a male or female name for most letters of the alphabet. Each new storm is given a name beginning with the next letter of the alphabet. Some hurricane names are used only once. A hurricane's name is not used again if the storm causes a lot of death and destruction. Andrew, Camille, Carmen, Donna, Bob, Mitch and Gilbert were killer hurricanes. Their names will never be used again. Different organizations around the world have their own systems for naming cyclones in their areas.

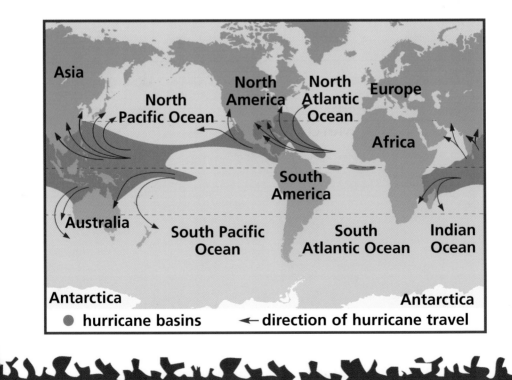

Asia

North Pacific Ocean

North America

North Atlantic Ocean

Europe

Africa

South America

Australia

South Pacific Ocean

South Atlantic Ocean

Indian Ocean

Antarctica

Antarctica

● hurricane basins   ← direction of hurricane travel

Where and when hurricanes form

Hurricanes start over warm, tropical water near the **equator**. The equator is an imaginary line around the centre of the Earth. It divides the Earth into two equal parts. A hurricane's strength depends on how warm the water is. The warmer the water gets, the stronger the hurricane will be. Tropical areas where many hurricanes begin are called hurricane basins.

North of the equator, the hurricane season lasts from May or June until November. Most hurricanes start between mid August and October. This is because ocean water is warmer during late summer and early autumn. The sun has heated the water all summer. South of the equator, off Australia and in the Indian Ocean, hurricanes are called tropical cyclones or typhoons. Most of these occur between November and March.

 This map shows where hurricanes begin.

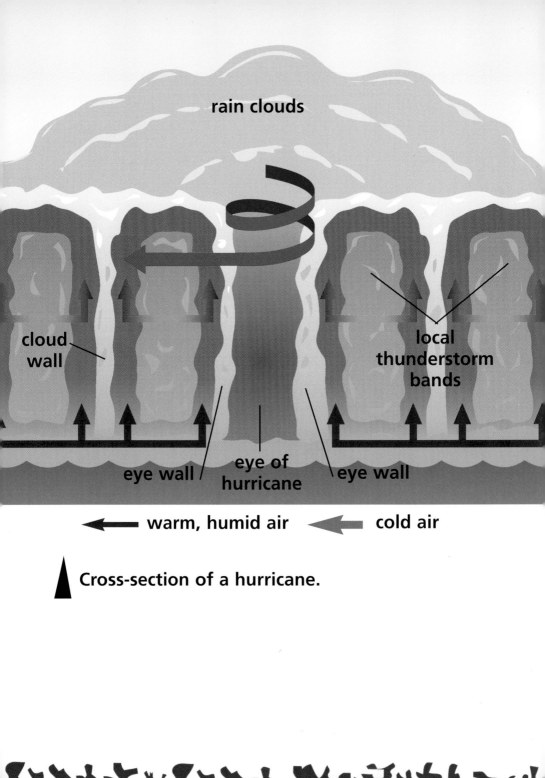

rain clouds

cloud wall

local thunderstorm bands

eye wall

eye of hurricane

eye wall

⬅ warm, humid air ⬅ cold air

▲ Cross-section of a hurricane.

A hurricane starts

Hurricanes start over warm ocean water. The warm water heats the air. This warm, **humid** air rises. Humid air contains a lot of water. The humid air cools as it rises and forms clouds. The clouds join together to cause thunderstorms. Wind blows the thunderstorms in a circle.

A storm becomes a hurricane or tropical cyclone when its winds reach 119 kilometres (74 miles) per hour. A hurricane's winds and its thunderstorms do not enter the **eye**. The eye is the centre of the hurricane.

A thick ring of clouds called the **eye wall** surrounds the eye. The eye wall is the strongest part of a hurricane. Winds blow fastest here. Heavy rain and strong thunderstorms come from its clouds.

Hurricanes can travel many kilometres a day. They stay strong as long as they are over warm ocean water. They may last for weeks. But most hurricanes last for about ten days.

After a while, hurricanes become weaker and turn into tropical storms. These storms can still cause many problems.

Surges and tornadoes

In the early 1900s, most death and damage caused by hurricanes came from **storm surges**. A storm surge is made up of huge, heavy waves. Winds from hurricanes push storm surges over land. Storm surges can wash away buildings and drown people.

Thunderstorms that make up a hurricane may start **tornadoes**. Tornadoes are violent, spinning wind funnels that rotate at up to 480 kilometres (300 miles) per hour. At ground level, the wind speed may be more than 500 kilometres per hour. Tornadoes can suck up or smash almost everything in their paths. Tornadoes that start over the ocean suck up water. They are called waterspouts. Most waterspouts lose their energy once they reach land.

 Many tornadoes start in hurricanes.

Hurricanes in history

Hurricanes are such powerful storms that they have changed history. One of the earliest recorded hurricanes hit Japan in 1281. At that time, the Mongol ruler Kublai Khan had sent a thousand warships to take over Japan. Japanese soldiers fought the Mongols for seven weeks and many died.

Then a hurricane blew in from the ocean. Its strong winds and rain sank most of the Mongol ships. More than 100,000 Mongol soldiers died.

Japanese people thanked their storm gods for the *kamikaze*. **Kamikaze** means 'divine wind from the gods'.

◀ **Hurricanes are powerful storms that can change history. This hurricane is causing coastal floods.**

Storm myths

In the past, people did not understand hurricanes. They told stories called myths to explain how hurricanes worked because they did not know the scientific explanations. In these stories, gods and goddesses were said to control the weather. People believed that these gods and goddesses sent hurricanes when people did bad things.

- **On islands in the Caribbean Sea,** the Carib Indians believed that an evil god called Hurican started storms. The word hurricane comes from this god's name.

- **In what is now Taiwan,** people believed in the wind god Hung Kong. They thought Hung Kong sent hurricanes from the China Sea. Hung Kong looked like a giant bird. The people said he flapped his wings to make hurricane winds.

Saffir-Simpson Scale

Scientists give each hurricane or tropical cyclone a number from the Saffir-Simpson Scale. This scale rates a hurricane based on how fast its winds blow. Hurricanes with the fastest winds cause the greatest damage.

	Winds	Storm surge	Damage
Category 1	119 to 153 km (74 to 95 miles) per hour	1 to 1.5 metres high	Some damage to trees and signs; coast roads flood
Category 2	154 to 177 km (96 to 110 miles) per hour	2 to 2.5 metres high	Medium damage to branches and street signs
Category 3	179 to 209 km (111 to 130 miles) per hour	3 to 3.5 metres high	Heavy damage to trees and roofs
Category 4	211 to 249 km (131 to 155 miles) per hour	4 to 5.5 metres high	Terrible damage to buildings and trees
Category 5	Winds faster than 249 km (155 miles) per hour	Higher than 5.5 metres	Buildings and trees ripped down

Galveston hurricane of 1900

On 8 September 1900, a hurricane hit Galveston, Texas, in the USA. Winds travelling at 210 kilometres (130 miles) per hour sent a 6-metre high storm surge through the town, smashing most of the buildings in its path.

One of the buildings nearest to the sea was an orphanage run by nuns. As the orphanage started to flood, the nuns used ropes to tie themselves to groups of children. They thought this would help them to save the children, but the flood water was too strong and fast. People found the nuns and children still tied together after the flood. They had all drowned.

This storm was the deadliest hurricane in US history. People were warned to go to high ground, but many stayed to watch the huge waves roll in. By the time the town started to flood, it was too late to escape. More than eight thousand people died within a few hours. Bodies floated in the water and hung in trees where the waves had swept them.

◄ A storm surge like this one destroyed Galveston.

EVACUATION
ROUTE

Hurricanes today

Today, scientists are learning a great deal about hurricanes. But science still has no way to stop hurricanes. Hurricanes damage property and can kill people.

In the early 1960s, the US government started the National Hurricane Centre in Miami, Florida. This centre is still in use today. There are tropical cyclone warning centres in other countries too, including Australia, Fiji and India. Scientists at the centres teach people how to protect themselves against hurricanes. Scientists warn people about approaching hurricanes. People then have time to **evacuate**. Evacuate means to leave quickly.

 A sign in the USA shows people where to go during a hurricane evacuation.

Bangladesh, 1991

On 30 April, 1991, a massive cyclone hit Bangladesh in southern Asia. Winds of more than 235 kilometres (145 miles) per hour lashed the south-eastern coast. A storm surge reaching 6 metres high destroyed almost everything in its path. Up to 10 million people were affected by the cyclone. More than 140,000 people died, 790,000 homes were destroyed and 9300 schools were destroyed or damaged.

Hurricane Andrew, 1992

In 1992, the National Hurricane Centre in the USA warned people about a strong hurricane called Andrew. It was heading for Florida and Louisiana. More than 1 million people evacuated the areas.

On 24 August, Hurricane Andrew slammed into southern Florida and Louisiana. Heavy rain and a storm surge caused flooding.

Hurricane Andrew destroyed thousands of buildings, including the National Hurricane Centre. It left many people homeless and killed 43 people. It cost more than any other hurricane in USA history.

◄ **Hurricane Andrew blew down trees and overturned cars.**

Hurricane Mitch, 1998

Mitch was the worst hurricane of 1998. This category-5 hurricane started near Jamaica in the Caribbean Sea. Its winds blew at more than 290 kilometres (180 miles) per hour.

Hurricane Mitch smashed into Honduras and Nicaragua in Central America. Up to 180 centimetres of rain fell. This caused major flooding and landslides. Water and mud destroyed roads and buildings. Whole villages slid down steep mountain sides. Hurricane Mitch caused millions of pounds worth of damage. It killed over 11,000 people and left more than 3 million without homes.

Cyclone Zoe, 2002

On 29 December, 2002, Cyclone Zoe, one of the strongest cyclones ever recorded, hit the Solomon Islands in the South Pacific Ocean. There were winds of up to 370 kilometres (230 miles) per hour. The island of Tikopia was the worst hit. The population of 1300 survived by hiding in ancient caves. Their homes and crops were destroyed.

 Hurricane Mitch did so much damage, scientists will not use the name again.

Hurricanes and science

Scientists can use new Doppler radar instruments to track hurricanes. Doppler radar machines measure wind speed and rainfall. Scientists also have **satellites** to help them. Satellites in orbit around the Earth take pictures of clouds and record wind speeds and send this information back to the Earth for scientists to study.

Hurricane hunters

Flying inside hurricanes is the best way to learn about them. Trained pilots and scientists fly aircraft into hurricanes. These people are called hurricane hunters.

◄ **Satellites take pictures of hurricanes. This is what a hurricane looks like from space.**

Hurricane hunters fly aircraft that have radar on them. Radar tells scientists about wind speed and rainfall in different parts of a hurricane. Hurricane hunters also drop probes into hurricanes. Probes are machines with computer chips inside them. As the probes fall, they record the wind speed in different parts of a storm. The probes send information back to the aircraft.

Watches, warnings and evacuations

Scientists do not know where and when a hurricane will hit until it is close to land. But they can now give people warning when hurricanes are about to strike.

Scientists give a hurricane or tropical cyclone watch if a hurricane or cyclone may reach land within 24 to 48 hours. People in the path of the hurricane should keep track of the weather. They should listen to radio and television news to get the latest advice.

Scientists give a hurricane or tropical cyclone warning when a hurricane or cyclone will definitely hit land within 24 hours. People must leave their homes if they are told to evacuate.

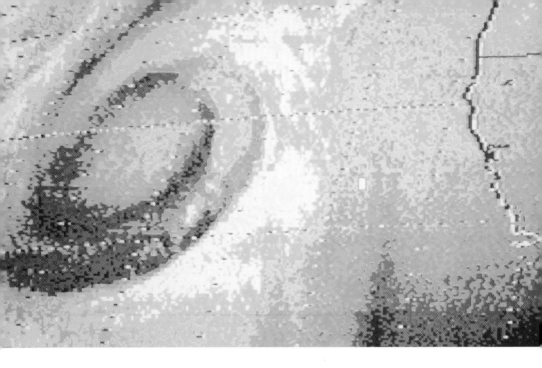

▲ **Radar tells scientists where hurricanes are.
Red areas show where heavy rain is falling.**

People can try to protect their property from
hurricanes before they evacuate. They can cover
their windows with boards and tie down anything
that might blow away. Stacking bags of sand
around houses helps to keep out flood water. In
areas where there are lots of hurricanes, people
can build storm shutters and strap their roofs to
the walls to make their houses stronger.

Hurricanes in the future

In the past, people have thought of many ways to stop hurricanes. Some scientists believed bombing hurricanes would stop them. They hoped the bombs would slow down the winds. Other scientists wanted to cool the ocean by floating large chunks of ice in them. Scientists have proved these ideas will not work. No one knows how to stop hurricanes.

Some scientists fear that the future will bring more hurricanes than ever. These scientists believe the Earth is getting warmer due to global warming. They fear hotter weather will make ocean water warmer. Warmer water could cause more and stronger hurricanes.

Each year, scientists learn more about hurricanes. They want to track hurricanes better. By doing this, they hope to save lives.

No one knows how to stop hurricanes from flooding land. Hurricane Floyd caused this flood in North Carolina, USA. ▶

Glossary

equator imaginary line around the centre of the Earth; the equator divides the Earth into two equal halves

evacuate to leave a place quickly to avoid danger

eye centre of a hurricane or tropical cyclone; the eye is calm and clear

eye wall ring of thick clouds that surrounds a hurricane or tropical cyclone's eye; the eye wall is the strongest part of the hurricane

humid air that contains lots of water

kamikaze Japanese word that means 'divine wind from the gods'

satellite equipment sent into space to circle the Earth; some satellites record information about the Earth

storm surge large ocean waves pushed over land by the wind of a hurricane or tropical cyclone

tornado spinning winds that blow at more than 400 kilometres (240 miles) per hour

tropical term used for hot areas near the equator

Addresses and Internet sites

Met Office
London Road
Bracknell
Berkshire, RG12 2SZ

Met Office Website
www.metoffice.gov.uk/education/curriculum/
  leaflets/hurricanes.html

Commonwealth Bureau of Meteorology
www.bom.gov.au/info/cyclone

Earth Observatory
www.earthobservatory.nasa.gov/NaturalHazards/

The Hurricane Hunters
www.hurricanehunters.com

National Hurricane Centre, USA
www.nhc.noaa.gov

Index

Australia 7, 19

Bangladesh 21

Carib Indians 14
China Sea 14
Cyclone Zoe 23

Doppler radar 25

evacuation 19, 21, 27
eye of the storm 9
eye wall 9

Honduras 23
Hung Kong 14
Hurican 14
Hurricane Andrew 6,
    21, 25
hurricane hunter 25, 26
Hurricane Mitch 6, 23
hurricane season 7

hurricane warning 26
hurricane watch 26

Jamaica 23
Japan 13

kamikaze 13
Kublai Khan 13

National Hurricane
    Centre, USA 19, 21
Nicaragua 23

satellite 25
Solomon Islands 23
storm surge 11, 17, 21

Taiwan 14
tornado 11
tropical storm 9